THE CHURCH
ON ITS KNEES

THE CHURCH ON ITS KNEES

Dynamic Prayer in the Local Church

JEREMY JENNINGS

Foreword by Sandy Millar

Alpha

Alpha Resources
Alpha North America

The Church on Its Knees

Front cover illustration by Charlie Mackesy.

ISBN: 1-931808-996

1 2 3 4 5 6 7 8 9 10 Printing/Year 08 07 06 05 04

Dedicated to the memory of my mother
Veronica Jennings (1923-1996)

Contents

Contents

Foreword

by Sandy Millar

It is strange in some ways that it has taken some of us so long, and I include myself in this, to discover in practice one of the most elementary principles of spiritual life. Thankfully though, the truth is dawning! The house of faith for which we all long and of which we are beginning to see such encouraging signs has as a main foundation—*prayer.*

In our own experience, God has released His Holy Spirit to give more of His people a fresh sense of urgency and desire to pray. In recent years, the corporate prayer meetings have grown substantially in our church and for much of that we have to thank Jeremy Jennings. With his own distinctive brand of humor and energy, he has brought enthusiasm and life to the church's responsibility to pray together. Creating interest and channeling the anointing that the Spirit has brought cannot in practice be easy. The church owes Jeremy and all who pray more than we will probably ever know. *The Church on its Knees* is primarily practical, and our hope is that it will enable every church to play a vital part in what God is building and, at the same time, enjoy it.

Sandy Millar
Holy Trinity Brompton

Introduction

"At that time people began to call on the name of the Lord." (Genesis 4: 26b)

On February 9, 1997 *The Sunday Telegraph* carried a full page article under the heading "The Church on its Knees." What followed was a gloomy report on the decline of church attendance and so on. When I saw it, the thought immediately struck me: *That's not the problem; it's the solution—THE CHURCH ON ITS KNEES!*

There is nothing new about a society, having turned its back on God, finding itself in decline. The history of Israel demonstrated this time and again, but so too does the post-war era in our own country. Church membership has fallen sharply, and the level of crime, for example, has soared. There are many people in our nation, especially among the young, who feel alienated, isolated, apathetic,

11

or angry. They are inclined not to vote or come to church because they question the point of everything, rebel against authority, and their frustration just increases. If ever there was a time for God's people to "call on the name of the Lord," it must be now. As we do so, we can lay the foundations for a healthier church and a healthier society.

In the coming chapters, I sometimes mention the number of people involved in prayer activities. I want to emphasize that at Holy Trinity Brompton (HTB), our central prayer meetings started in 1990 with only a handful of people getting together once a week. Although the numbers have grown substantially since then, not every meeting is as well attended or goes as well as we would like. Nor does every prayer apparently receive an immediate answer. Ours is but one experience, and this is not the only approach. However, I want to encourage anyone thinking about starting a new program of prayer in their church to do so and to trust God with the outcome. We have found that He has led us from one stage to the next along the way. We have also found that praying together is vital to our well-being and effectiveness as a church.

I would like to acknowledge the debt we owe

to the many people who were praying at HTB before the current meetings began. And I want to thank all those who have worked with me in the development of our corporate prayer since then. Without them, and without those who have faithfully supported the prayer meetings, there would have been no story to tell. I am also very grateful to everyone who has been involved in the writing and production of this book. Last, but by no means least, I want to thank my wife, Milly, and our children for their love and support throughout.

CHAPTER 1

What Is Prayer About?

"And when you pray . . ." (Matthew 6:5a)

Like every Christian I know, I have always thought prayer was a good idea, but it has taken me a long time to see how much depends on it. Like the air we breathe, it is easily taken for granted, but its effects are felt in every area of life. On one level, Christians pray because they see in their own experience, and in the experience of others, that prayer brings results. But on another level we learn that it is one of the main ways of developing the deep relationship with the Father for which we all long.

In Romans 8, Paul talks of the Spirit testifying that we are God's children: "by him we cry, 'Abba, Father,'" (v. 15b). He goes on to say, "the Spirit helps us in our weakness. We do not know what we ought to pray for, but the Spirit himself intercedes with groans that words cannot express," (v. 26). So, on the one hand, the Spirit draws us into God's family circle and, on the other, He helps us with what to say when we get there. In this sense, He does it all but *we still have to respond by praying*.

Hebrews 7:25 speaks of Jesus as one who is "able to save completely those who come to God through him, because he always lives to intercede for them." It is amazing to think that Jesus is praying *for us* right now and always. The aim of our prayers should be to enter into the divine dialogue that is already taking place. With the Spirit's help, we ought to seek to listen and then join in by agreeing with what we hear. In this way, prayer draws us into relationship with the Trinity, and it only becomes truly effective as it flows in that context.

God's Presence

Moses enjoyed one of the most profound relationships with God ever known. "The Lord would speak to Moses face to face, as one speaks to a friend," (Exodus 33:11a). In the same chapter we learn that Moses prayed: "If your Presence does not go with us, do not send us up from here. How will anyone know that you are pleased with me and with your people unless you go with us? What else will distinguish me and your people from all the other people on the face of the earth?" (vs. 15-16).

There is passion in Moses' words. For him, this issue of the manifest presence of God was more precious than life itself; without God, he and his people were lost—no different from anyone else. In fact, their plight would have been worse because they would have lost a presence they had once enjoyed. This was the distinguishing characteristic that marked them out from the other peoples of their time. Why should it be different for the people of God today?

Suppose Moses and his people had gone on without God. They would have become people who knew about God without actually knowing Him—a terrible state. What a tragedy that would have been, and what parallel dangers we in the church face today. Important though it is, our theology alone won't satisfy us. We need to be in relationship with God. When we are on our knees praying, we are actively participating in that relationship—who we are before God is truly who we are. Fortunately God's answer to Moses brought him the comfort he sought: "And the Lord said to Moses, 'I will do the very thing you have asked, because I am pleased with you and I know you by name,'" (Exodus 33:17).

I have come to see that this is the heart of the matter. Whatever else it is, prayer is communicating with God. So when we pray, either alone or with others, we are dependent on His presence. We must pray for the same answer that God gave Moses. I would rather leave a prayer meeting knowing that we had been in the presence of God than being aware that a long list of needs had been systematically presented. Answers to prayer should be seen as flowing from a living relationship with our loving heavenly Father. After all, as Jesus tells us in Matthew 6:8, God knows what we need before we ask Him.

One of the greatest calls to prayer is given in 2 Chronicles 7:14. The full text is reproduced at the beginning of the next chapter, where it is considered more fully. It includes God's invitation to "seek my face." I have often overlooked this and concentrated more on the other directives in the verse, but to do so is to miss an essential point. What a privilege it is to be invited to seek the face of God. What a call to intimacy—and this from the pages of the Old Testament. Moses sought this depth of relationship, and he pleased God. How much more should we, who live under the new covenant, do the same? The writer to the Hebrews encourages us, "Let us then approach the throne of grace with confidence, so that we may receive mercy and find grace to help us in our time of need," (Hebrews 4:16). Jesus has given us access to the Father and, with the Spirit's help, that is where prayer should take us.

Of course there is always work to be done, but our first priority should be to come into the presence of God. This is where our deepest needs will be met, and where we will receive the direction we seek. Prayer can be a long monologue, but it ought to be much more, and then it becomes exciting. We need to explore what it means to seek God's face, trying out different methods of worship and learning how to wait on the Lord and hear from Him. This should come before our needs and wants. In fact, the need above all needs is to know God. For Moses this knowledge immediately preceded one of the greatest moments of self-revelation by God. The passage in Exodus 33 concludes with him being shown the glory of the Lord from a cleft in a rock.

Realizing the potential of prayer must involve seeking to grasp what it meant for

Moses to be in that cleft. We have had some wonderful answers to prayer, and we praise God for that. The exponential growth of the Alpha course[1], a fresh outpouring of the Spirit and the churches planted over the past few years are all examples. But more than anything else, we have come to value time spent in the Lord's presence both individually and corporately. David put it like this: "One thing I ask of the Lord, this is what I seek: that I may dwell in the house of the Lord all the days of my life, to gaze upon the beauty of the Lord and to seek him in his temple," (Psalm 27:4).

God's Power

I often tell the story of a man who came to one of the conferences at HTB and told me about the "Prayer Weeks" in his church. Although they longed for growth as a church, none had been forthcoming. Then they had the idea of canceling all their other midweek activities and meeting to pray instead for one week. From that time, their church started to grow and every time they have repeated the exercise it has grown further.

One of the defining characteristics of the church in Acts was its dependence on prayer;

there are twenty-six direct references to it throughout the book. Clearly, the early church was a praying church. It was not just that they prayed when they were in trouble, although they did that too. For example, they prayed in anticipation of the day of Pentecost (Acts 1:14), and they also prayed when King Herod had Peter put in prison (Acts 12:5). Indeed, Peter interrupted the very prayer meeting that had brought about his miraculous escape by arriving at the house where his friends were still praying!

Throughout the book, we see groups and individuals turning to prayer in a whole variety of circumstances because it was part of their way of life. Acts 2:42 tells us of the believers in those days: "They devoted themselves to the apostles' teaching and to the fellowship, to the breaking of bread and to prayer." Praying was not the only thing they did, but it was a central activity. Their experience was that it was effective, time and again.

When Peter and John were released after imprisonment and interrogation before the Sanhedrin, the church faced a crisis, which is recorded in Acts 4. Speaking or teaching in the name of Jesus had been forbidden by the authorities. Had Jesus' followers obeyed, their cause would have been lost but, instead, we are told, "When they heard this, they [the people] raised their voices together in prayer to God," (v. 24a). Their spontaneous response was to pray. Part of their prayer was, "Now, Lord, consider their threats and enable your servants to speak your word with great boldness. Stretch out your hand to heal and perform miraculous signs and wonders through the name of your holy servant Jesus," (vs. 29-30). Afterward "they were all filled with the Holy Spirit and spoke the word of God boldly," (v. 31b) and, as far as we can tell, they continued to do so for the rest of their lives.

The final sentence in the Book of Acts speaks of Paul under house arrest: "Boldly and without hindrance he preached the kingdom of God and taught about the Lord Jesus Christ," (Acts 28: 31). Evidently, the prayer for boldness, prayed all those years earlier, was still working. Paul was undaunted by the threat of secular authority. Furthermore, the whole book is a continual record of God intervening with "miraculous signs and wonders" mentioned in that same prayer of Acts 4.

When the early church prayed, it worked, and we need to learn that lesson again today.

God can change the current situation. Our

churches could be full again and there could be a time when we have to plant and build new ones. Once more, the church could be the salt and light of our society; its voice could be heard and heeded by a population seeking moral guidance and leadership. But none of this will happen if we do not pray.

Note

1. The Alpha course began at HTB about twenty years ago. It is a basic introduction to the Christian faith and there are now approximately 10,000 such courses running around the world.

CHAPTER 2

What Makes for Effective Prayer and Fasting?

"When I shut up the heavens so that there is no rain, or command locusts to devour the land or send a plague among my people, if my people, who are called by my name, will humble themselves and pray and seek my face and turn from their wicked ways, then will I hear from heaven and will forgive their sin and will heal their land." (2 Chronicles 7:13-14)

Praying Alone

Throughout the Bible, those men and women who were greatly used by God were also people of prayer. Look at Moses, Daniel, Esther, David, or Paul, for instance, not to mention Jesus' own example. Prayer, as Bishop Lesslie Newbigin said, is "the distinctive resource of the believer." Furthermore, healthy individual prayer is essential for the development of effective corporate prayer. One of my favorite examples of it comes from the life of Isaac.

We read in Genesis 25:21, "Isaac prayed to the Lord on behalf of his wife, because she was barren. The Lord answered his prayer, and his wife Rebekah became pregnant." Not everyone turns to God in difficult circumstances. One of the things that marked Isaac out was that he did. In our church, I remember Pastor John Wimber praying for someone who had been diagnosed as medically incapable of conception. Nine months later, her first child was born. Since then, four more have followed (and her husband has been ordained as a minister in the Church of England!).

In 1 Chronicles 4:9-10, we encounter an unusual biblical example of personal prayer in the person of Jabez. Of him we are told: "Jabez was more honorable than his brothers. His mother had named him Jabez, saying, 'I gave birth to him in pain.' Jabez cried out to the God of Israel, 'Oh, that you would bless me and enlarge my territory! Let your hand be with me, and keep me from harm so that I will be free from pain.' And God granted his request." He prays the kind of prayer to which we can all relate, though we might hesitate to use it! Nevertheless, he was described as "more honorable than his brothers," and we are told ınat "God granted his request." Evidently, one of the things that marked Jabez out from those around him was his prayer life.

I had a similar experience of prayer in 1982. My brother-in-law owns a garage and was facing a crisis as the economy was in a recession and new car sales had completely collapsed. It was obvious that the business would fail unless the situation improved, so we decided to pray (he had already tried everything else!). We agreed to be specific and pray for six cars to be sold in the coming month of July.

I had never prayed for anything so urgently before, and the sales came one by one. We watched (and prayed) as the transformation occurred. Six new cars were sold and, right at the end of the month, a seventh! I have always seen that last one as a special gift and encouragement from God. Within a period of months, the business was restored and, since then, it has developed with the opening of two new branches. As the crisis passed, so did the urgency to pray, but I have never doubted that God answered our prayers and saved the day.

There is no reason to suppose that Isaac or Jabez found it any easier to pray than we do. But they overcame the barriers that erect themselves against praying. Even at this basic level of need-driven and self-centered prayer, there is an acknowledgment that God exists, is sovereign, and holds the answers to our needs. It also involves an acceptance that there are areas of our lives beyond our control, and that entails humility. We need to learn that our responsibility is to pray and then to trust God with the outcome.

Very often, prayer will begin at this level before it develops further. As we start to experience some answers to prayer, it is natural for thanksgiving to become part of the dialogue. We should also learn to incorporate praise, repentance, contemplation, and listening, and many find the gift of tongues invaluable as part of their prayer lives. Praying does not need to be complicated. I once heard of a man who would spend long periods sitting in a church staring at a stained glass window depicting an image of Jesus. When someone asked him what he was doing, he replied, "I look at Him and He looks at me." But there is one thing that all prayer does require, which is *time*, and that may involve an alarm clock!

Praying Together

At the beginning of the Book of Acts, we are

told: "On one occasion, while he [Jesus] was eating with them [the apostles], he gave them this command: 'Do not leave Jerusalem, but wait for the gift my Father promised, which you have heard me speak about. For John baptized with water, but in a few days you will be baptized with the Holy Spirit,'" (Acts 1:4-5). Then on the day of Pentecost the Holy Spirit came and filled them, Peter addressed the crowd, and thousands were converted. But remember! The disciples had been told to *wait.*

What did they do during that time? Acts 1:14 tells us, "they all joined together constantly in prayer." They did not think it sufficient merely to go to Jerusalem and wait, even though that was all Jesus apparently required of them. They prayed together. They had witnessed the power of the Holy Spirit in Jesus' life, and they must have longed for the same in their own.

The group of men and women who prayed while they waited were the same people involved in the explosive evangelism on the Day of Pentecost and beyond. For them, the work of prayer and the work of building the church were seen as woven together. It should be the same for us. We need dynamic prayer undergirding the work of the church today.

Our experience confirms that, numerically speaking, a church's prayer meeting will draw in about ten percent of its wider membership. Of course, this requires a committed pool of more than that, because not everyone can come to every meeting.

In a way, praying together is like the tip of the iceberg in that it is the public expression of the activity. Its base is all the private and other less visible prayer taking place. Nevertheless, the healthy expression of corporate prayer was part of the life of the early church and it needs to be part of its life again today.

There are thousands of churches in our country. If growing numbers of them started seeing ten percent of their members praying together regularly, it would surely have an impact. This seems an achievable target for churches to work toward. Furthermore, as they and their communities began to change, the momentum of prayer would gather and numbers should increase. If each church that became involved represented a light, the process could quickly lead to light spreading across the country.

Glenda Waddell works as personal assistant to Sandy Millar (vicar of HTB). She has been involved in the corporate prayer at HTB from an early stage. We now lead one of the church's regular prayer meetings together, and this is her account of how the activity has built up since it started.

To allow more people to come, we started a new meeting at 7:30 a.m. on Thursdays. I was involved with that from the outset. We began by meeting for thirty minutes, but the time went so quickly that we decided to start earlier and increase it to an hour. Immediately the numbers doubled! The prayer was always interspersed with worship. We experimented with different models of prayer. There was unity. There was commitment. There was excitement at being involved in what God was doing. We saw gifts released. Our faith grew. What many of us had feared might be a dull meeting turned out to be a highlight of the week.

After a challenging sermon on prayer, the numbers redoubled. New morning prayer meetings were started on Tuesdays and, eventually, on Wednesdays as well. As time went by, there were other initiatives: prayer weekends, nights of prayer, and a special excursion to pray for London on a

Thames river boat! And all the time more people became involved.

Looking back, I think it is possible to see the way that God has "grown the prayer" in order to "grow the work." When the prayer life of the church began to grow, I don't think anyone could have imagined the way that the Alpha course would expand. Now we can see how key the prayer has been. I once sensed God say: "The only number I won't multiply is zero!" That means that every "pray-er" and every prayer counts. I find that immensely encouraging!

Praying for the Nation

This chapter began with the text: "... if my people, who are called by my name, will humble themselves and pray and seek my face and turn from their wicked ways, then will I hear from heaven and will forgive their sin and will heal their land," (2 Chronicles 7:13-14). We are told that God spoke these words to Solomon at the time of the opening and dedication of the temple in Jerusalem. The setting was one of national peace and prosperity with an extraordinary manifestation of the Lord's

presence and pleasure with His people.
Nevertheless, we see God looking ahead to
darker days, and giving His prescription for
what they should do then.

We see God addressing the people called by
His name. Today, that must refer to the
Christian church. We need to acknowledge that
only God has the answers to the problems that
face us nationally, and we must urgently turn
to Him in prayer. On the basis of the above text,
I see revival as being a process culminating in
a "healing of the land." Our society needs
change, and there is no evidence of any revival
beginning without prayer.

In 1857, New York was in the midst of a
national disaster. A financial crash had ruined
many of its one-million population. On July 1,
Jeremiah Lanphier, a middle-aged businessman, took up an appointment as a missionary
in the city center. He decided to start a lunch-
time prayer meeting. On the first week, he
prayed alone for half an hour until five others
joined him. The following week twenty came.
Within six months, the meeting spread and
10,000 people came daily to pray and a revival
in North America had begun.

We have found at HTB that what began as
an idea to pray together for the Sunday services

in 1990 has developed into a growing urgency to pray for revival. As Billy Graham has said, the three keys to revival are: *prayer, prayer, prayer.*

Fasting

We should remember that Jesus fasted as part of the preparation for His life's work (Matthew 4:2). And frequently in the Bible, we see the people of God turning to fasting often in difficult circumstances. If the situation is serious, we need to confront it accordingly. At one level, fasting can involve forgoing one meal or forsaking something else for a limited period. As we know from Jesus' life, the other end of the scale is not to eat for forty days.

People should not fast if that would be medically unsuitable (such as during pregnancy) and should not do so in ways that interfere with their existing commitments or damage their health. Nevertheless, Jesus said "when" and not "if" you fast (Matthew 6: 16). Fasting is an important Christian discipline which, when allied with prayer, is bound to reinforce it. It is better to start small and build up the activity gradually, learning from experience.

Fasting Alone

I have found it helpful to include fasting in my own life for a particular purpose such as guidance, or for a defined goal such as the healing of a friend. Equally, if we know there is some aspect of our lives which is not right in God's sight, I strongly recommend the discipline. For me, the practice has involved fasting from food for periods ranging from one meal to several days, and giving up other things for longer periods. I have never found it easy, but it has enabled me to hear God more clearly and helped me to develop a deeper relationship with Him.

Having observed several people who fast regularly, I have seen a growing effectiveness develop in their lives. A good example is someone with whom I work closely. In 1997, she felt it would be right to fast for a total of forty days in response to a call from God. This entailed three consecutive days for eleven months and one seven-day fast during the year. She is closely involved with the introduction of the Alpha course in many prisons and it is now running in over half of them nationally.

Suppose, as individual Christians, some of us decided to develop the practice of missing a meal and praying instead, say, once a week? The prayer could be about personal, local church, or wider issues—including national ones. This, like the idea of more churches seeing ten percent of their members praying together regularly, seems an attainable target. Of course, many may fast and pray more than this already but, if not, why not consider it? No one will die of starvation as a result! If the idea really took off, the results could be very exciting.

Fasting Together

We are naturally cautious about imposing fasting on people, although we do believe it has a place. For example, as the prayer leadership team, we decided to fast at our Tuesday lunch-time meetings (these are referred to in chapter 4). We miss the sandwiches, but we have felt better able to discern God's will and guidance in this way. We also believe this has been a small way of showing God that we are seriously concerned to see the development of corporate prayer at HTB. And it has allowed more time for praying together at the meetings!

As a church, we have encouraged corporate fasting, for example, during a day of prayer for revival and it is included in our Prayer Weekends. These are described in chapter 7.

An example of fasting in the national context occurred when the country was faced with the threat of invasion by the French in 1756, and George II called for a day of prayer and fasting. John Wesley recorded in his journal on Friday, February 6: "The fast-day was a glorious day, such as London has scarcely ever seen since the Restoration. Every church in the city was more than full, and a solemn seriousness sat on every face. Surely God heareth the prayer, and there will yet be a lengthening of our tranquillity." In a footnote he wrote, "Humility was turned into national rejoicing for the threatened invasion by the French was averted."

Like then, it seems that only a monarch (in conjunction with the government and national church leaders) could issue a call to pray and fast on this scale today. Nevertheless, we should seek to promote this as part of the process of national revival and to encourage it among churches.

Repentance and Persistence

Without repentance, it is unlikely that effective prayer or fasting will take place at all. When

Jesus taught His disciples to pray, He induded the words: "Forgive us our debts, as we also have forgiven our debtors," (Matthew 6:12). The only thing He went on to say after completing the prayer was, "For if you forgive others when they sin against you, your heavenly Father will also forgive you. But if you do not forgive others their sins, your Father will not forgive your sins," (vs. 14-15).

If there is any unforgiveness in us, we need to deal with it or it will block our prayers. Of course, this applies to other unconfessed sin as well. It does not matter how earnestly, long or loud we pray; if we are in the wrong place with God, we need to deal with that first. The requirements of us in 2 Chronicles 7: 14 include repentance. The people had to "turn from their wicked ways" before God promised to hear them, forgive them, and heal them. Effective prayer and fasting must always include sincere repentance backed up by appropriate action where necessary.

In prayer meetings, saying the Confession together, perhaps followed by a period of silence, can be very effective. For ease of reference, this is reproduced below:

Almighty God, our Heavenly Father, we

*have sinned against You and against other
people, in thought and word and deed,
through negligence, through weakness,
through our own deliberate fault. We are
truly sorry and repent of all our sins. For
the sake of Your Son Jesus Christ, who
died for us, forgive us all that is past; and
grant that we may serve You in newness of
life, to the glory of Your name. Amen.*

It is helpful to remind people in this
context that "If we confess our sins, he [God]
is faithful and just and will forgive us our sins
and purify us from all unrighteousness," (1
John 1:9). Then we can proceed, trusting in
these words.

Such repentance needs to be inspired by the
Holy Spirit, who will convict but not condemn
us. Any form of division or disunity in the
church should be addressed urgently. Jesus'
prayer for all believers in John 17:20-26 reveals
how important this is to Him.

In Luke's account of the teaching of the
Lord's Prayer, we see Jesus emphasizing
persistence in prayer (Luke 11:1-8). And the
reason He told His disciples the parable of the
persistent widow was "to show them that they
should always pray and not give up," (Luke

18:1). For prayer to be effective, it is essential to persevere when necessary. Praying for revival certainly falls into this category.

CHAPTER 3

What about Praying Together?

"They all joined together constantly in prayer . . ."
(Acts 1:14a)

Is Praying Together Necessary?

People need to see the point of any activity if they are to support it. Corporate prayer is no exception. When we pray privately, much of our prayer is quite properly self-centered. When we pray together, the agenda becomes a common one. One of the things I love the most about praying with others is just that. I can come to the meeting and, for a period of time, focus on issues of joint concern. Thus unity is developed and any personal preoccupations are seen in a better perspective or can disappear altogether!

We have already considered various examples of the early church praying together in the Book of Acts. We need to see this in its biblical perspective and act accordingly in the church today. For us, an important step was to start a one-hour prayer meeting on Thursdays. Regular meetings of this type have since developed into the main expression of corporate prayer at HTB. Of course, these operate alongside and reinforce other corporate prayer such as in the services and home groups.

Content

The content of the central prayer meetings has changed as we have progressed. Our aim has been to keep in step with God's Spirit. We have learned that He may keep us praying for "home" issues, or He may prompt us to include wider ones. Usually it is both. We now have four one-hour prayer meetings a week, and each one is flexible, but they are focused as follows:

1. Mission (Tuesday at 7:00 a.m.)
2. Family life (Wednesday at 7:00 a.m.)
3. Church life at HTB (Thursday at 7:00 a.m.)
4. Revival (Thursday at 7:00 p.m.)

While each meeting has its specific focus, our policy is to include any major issues for prayer as they arise. For example, we often pray for peace in Northern Ireland, especially when something important has been reported in the news that could affect the well-being of the peace process there.

One of the most important activities to include is thanksgiving and praise to God, and we always start with worship. When Jesus healed ten men of leprosy, only one returned to thank Him (Luke 17:15-16). Whatever the reasons, the others failed to do so, and Jesus found their omission disturbing. We need to avoid the same mistake. It can be a good idea for the leader of a meeting to include a report of answers to previous prayer in his or her opening remarks. This can then lead into a time of specific thanks and more praise. Starting meetings on this note also raises faith in those present before they pray about other issues. Worshiping God during them helps maintain the right attitude of heart as they proceed.

Wherever possible, we try and pray *for* people and things (and not against them) to avoid negativity. For example, prayer about child abuse can be focused on the protection and healing of the children concerned and, even in these shocking circumstances, we can pray that those responsible may be changed by the love of God.

A sample program for a one-hour prayer meeting is shown below:

PROGRAM	MINUTES
Opening worship	10
Leader's introduction—intended to inspire those present to pray more effectively (including any feedback concerning answered prayer from previous meeting(s)/ thanksgiving to God)	5
Prayer for:	
• Church leader and family	5
• Worship	5
• Forthcoming services	5
• Alpha "at home" and in other churches	5
• Worship	5
• Overseas project, such as wo rk with street children in Brazil (perhaps preceded by interview with someone directly involved)	5(+)
• Worship	5(-)
• Other churches and leaders	5
• Lord's prayer/closing worship	5
	60

Promotion

No one will come to a meeting if they do not know about it. Several times a year, we hold "Prayer Sundays" when we make the need for corporate prayer the main focus of the services throughout the day. The sermons are usually given by a leader who is directly involved, perhaps including an interview with a regular participator. We devote time to praying, using one or more of the models described in chapter 6. This has proved an effective means of promotion. It has given people a taste of what they can expect in the prayer meetings and, in that way, encourages them to come.

Other means of promotion include flyers and verbal notices in services, and word of mouth. We need them all! I also write a regular article on prayer in our church's monthly newspaper.

Timing

It is important to consider carefully what time of day would suit your members best. We started with an evening meeting, but soon added one in the morning because others found that more convenient. We have two important rules for prayer meetings: start on time and stop on time. People who have been made late for work or an appointment by a meeting that overran are unlikely to return.

Leadership

At the risk of stating the obvious, the leader needs to lead. But he or she needs to seek the guidance of the Holy Spirit both before and during the meeting. Ideally, every prayer meeting leader should be supported by a team that meets regularly and is mutually accountable. Leadership is the subject of chapter 4.

Worship and Variety

Worship and variety are both crucial in prayer meetings. Worship and prayer can be combined very effectively, and we often intercede by singing one of the many songs that are prayers in themselves. This is covered in chapter 5. Chapter 6 considers different ways of praying together.

Unity

Unity is both essential for, and a benefit of, prayer meetings. When we pray with others we are drawn together in a common cause. The key is aligning ourselves with God's will. Our involvement is essentially being obedient to Him. This vertical and horizontal unity is vital for effective corporate prayer.

People

Finally, every prayer meeting needs the presence of God and the presence of His people. Both are essential. Jesus has promised to be there when we meet in His name even in small numbers (Matthew 18:20). There is a recurrent theme in Scripture that God will only act when He finds the response He is looking for in us. Below, in their own words, are some of the reasons why people come to the meetings at HTB:

1. I have never felt that I have done anything particularly special for Jesus in response to what He has done for me. But I do know that without prayers for the blessing and protection of the people and activities that we believe are important to the kingdom, our efforts would surely fail. If any minuscule contribution can help, then it's the least I can do to get up and be there! (Salesman)

2. I have found my own regular prayers strengthened and my prayer horizon widened.

The "report back" of prayers being answered is exciting and moving, and I never cease to be amazed and thankful by what can be done by prayer. (Architect)

3. *I enjoy the fellowship, friendship, and unity that are so prevalent at the meetings. There is a great sense that we are in this together, doing the best we can, often feeling hopelessly inadequate, but like children beseeching a loving and faithful parent. It is challenging and humbling but also exhilarating and deeply rewarding.* (Businessman)

4. *I started attending the prayer meetings and found so much to enjoy there. The worship is absolutely wonderful and it is very exciting to see and hear how God is moving as a result of prayer. It is so typical of God that, while we go to pray for the things that are on His heart, we find that He is no man's debtor. I always leave a prayer meeting feeling really blessed and encouraged and full of energy!* (Saleswoman)

5. *I love praying alone but it is also great to pray with the church family.* (Artist)

6. *Prayer provides such a wonderful*

opportunity for individuals to be involved in all areas of the church's life ... I think that the more we pray, the more our desire to pray increases. (Law Student)

7. *I had no idea praying could be so much fun (especially at 7:00 in the morning!). I don't want to romanticize the meetings—there are some times when it is hard work—but what better way to spend your energies than praying through the issues that are on God's heart?* (Student)

CHAPTER 4

What about Leading Meetings?

*A voice says, "Cry out."And I said,
"What shall I cry?"* (Isaiah 40:6a)

The church should develop and maintain
corporate prayer as one of its chief activities. To
do so, it needs leaders who will release and
facilitate this activity under the guidance and
leadership of the Holy Spirit. Moreover, if this
is to be achieved, churches will probably need
to appoint one leader responsible for prayer
and, in due course, he or she will benefit from
the support of a leadership team. This person
need not be the leader of the church but is, of
course, acting under their authority. Nor is it
necessary for the leadership team to be paid
staff.

Preparation

I currently lead an early morning meeting. I used to endeavor to stay in bed as late as possible. Once I had perfected the art, I could set the alarm for 6:30 a.m. and be leading the meeting at 7:00 a.m.! However, I soon discovered that it does not work. It becomes obvious that you have been cutting corners and *you* know that you are running the meeting on low spiritual reserves.

Preparing Oneself

Reading God's word and praying alone are at the root of the leadership of corporate prayer. For how long? At present, I allow about an hour before the meeting, but different lengths of time will suit different people. Whatever it is, it ought to be part of a regular discipline of personal prayer in our lives, and should not take place only in preparation for a meeting. The leader should practice in private what he or she preaches in public. There is definitely a link between the private and public aspects of leadership.

Preparation of Agenda

I reach the church at least fifteen minutes

before the meeting starts and put the final touches to the agenda then. Ideally, I will have met with my co-leader a day or so before the meeting in order to discuss topical issues and to allow a provisional agenda to begin to build up in my mind.

Leading

A prayer meeting benefits from clearly defined leadership and when the leader is in a partnership of trust with the people who come to pray. He or she is a facilitator who aims to foster a sense of unity, openness, and mutual encouragement. While trying not to talk too much, the leader should exhort with sensitivity, humor and passion. The aim is for a natural flow from topic to topic and from worship to prayer. A good analogy is that of the conductor of an orchestra whose ability and clear directives should draw out and develop the potential of everyone involved.

We should aim to work through the prepared agenda while remaining open to the promptings and leadership of the Holy Spirit. Some of the best meetings, in my experience, are when the Holy Spirit has overtaken our earlier plans. Then everyone senses that God is really at work. Very occasionally, the leader may need to take a stand, tactfully but firmly. Someone may try to introduce a new and unhelpful direction to a meeting and it is necessary then for the leader to impose his or her authority as diplomatically as possible. Leaders should remember that common sense is one of their principal assets and that their first impressions are normally correct!

Spiritual Dynamic

Praying is a spiritual activity, and it is therefore wise to expect the enemy to oppose it. We are entirely dependent on God's help and protection. From time to time, difficulties can arise ranging from trivial misunderstandings to more serious problems. If someone becomes a distraction to others, then it is right to confront them and, as a last resort, prevent them from coming. It was a great help when I was praying about one such situation and sensed the Lord saying, "You mind the prayers, I will mind the 'pray-ers.'" The person concerned never came again. We should not forget to turn to God when help is needed.

Prophecy

First, what do we mean by prophecy?

Obviously, it is impossible to give a full definition here, but I take it to mean: God's character and ways as revealed in Scripture being applied in the local context by the direct action of the Spirit. It is often expressed through some words, an impression, or a picture, and it should be welcomed with open arms. Paul tells us to "eagerly desire spiritual gifts, especially the gift of prophecy," (1 Corinthians 14:1). He also says, "Do not put out the Spirit's fire; do not treat prophecies with contempt," (1 Thessalonians 5:19-20). Like all the gifts, prophecy is given for the common good and should be encouraged and well managed. The leader's job is to facilitate the activity, but also to be clear with those involved that they are accountable in the use of their prophetic gifts.

On the above basis, it becomes far easier to welcome prophecy at appropriate points during a meeting, including setting aside time to wait on God for the purpose. If the person who has spoken a prophetic word is a sincere Christian, we should listen carefully. Such inspiration can galvanize us in our efforts, help to channel our prayers more specifically, and reassure us that we are on the right track as we pray.

I often remind people of Paul's words from

1 Corinthians 14:3: "But those who prophesy speak to people for their strengthening, encouragement, and comfort." It is a good test, and my experience is that authentic prophecy will always strike such a chord with those to whom it is addressed. We are looking for the kind of prophecy that builds up the church. Prayer meetings should be an ideal forum for its development because of the unity and trust among those involved.

One of the central roles of such revelation is to inspire and sustain intercession. We looked in chapter 2 at what the disciples did, according to the Book of Acts, between Jesus revealing that they were to receive the gift of the Holy Spirit and the Day of Pentecost when the Spirit came. They prayed.

Some time ago, in our context, someone had a picture of five alarm clocks. We took that as being the Lord's encouragement for us to work toward having a prayer meeting on every weekday morning and we are now well on the way to reaching that target. (We decided to disregard the less helpful interpretation offered that it might relate to how many alarm clocks we need to wake up in time to pray!)

Of course, misuse of the gift of prophecy needs to be restrained. In our experience, people who come regularly to prayer meetings need very little assessing, especially those who have demonstrated their commitment by coming at 7:00 a.m.! The leader will very quickly get to know the regular "pray-ers." The weighing and testing of prophecy has much to do with being sure of the character of those concerned. We are looking for prayerful people who have put behind them the desire to appear to be something they are not, and who are not dogmatic or "heavy" in their tone. Remember, if prophecy is true, it loses nothing by being tested along the lines described.

In larger meetings, it can be helpful to provide pens and paper for people to write down their impressions and to hand them to one of the leaders. The leader is then responsible for deciding if and when to use the material publicly. Whether used in the meeting or not, the papers are always collected and kept for future reference.

Leading in Teams

A leader and a worship leader form the nucleus of a leadership team. As corporate prayer develops in the life of a church, co-leaders will emerge, and this is a process to be encouraged. Working with a team means bigger things can

be attempted. Here are some suggested
guidelines.

- Aim to meet regularly as a team. We meet
  for an hour each Tuesday at lunch time.
- Use the meeting to pray for each other, to
  brainstorm, to hear reports from different
  meetings, and to consider future plans.
- It can be good to fast together.
- A team lightens the load. For example, it
  is much better to subdivide long meetings
  into shorter periods and to appoint
  different leaders for each section. (I have
  twice led four-hour prayer meetings by
  myself, but I never want to do it again!)
  Different voices and styles add variety. We
  also run our weekly meetings with joint
  leaders wherever possible. Apart from
  anything else, it is much more fun
  working as a team; one of our team
  members still holds first prize for the best
  excuse for arriving late at any meeting,
  when she announced that her daughter's
  guinea pig had escaped in the car on the
  way in!

CHAPTER 5

What about Worship?

"Enter his gates with thanksgiving and his courts with praise; give thanks to him and praise his name."
(Psalm 100:4)

Although the full implications of worshiping God are obviously wider, the focus of this chapter is music and singing in the context of a prayer meeting. When we first started meeting regularly, we did so without them. We soon realized that this was a mistake and began to include singing. This quickly revealed the need for a worship leader! Thankfully, one was found, and since then more have followed.

We have learned that worship and prayer complement and enhance each other. We have also found that a prayer meeting is an ideal setting for experimentation in the area of worship. This has led to a contribution to the

wider life of the church as new styles and
giftings have developed. Without the worship, I
have no doubt that our prayer meetings would
quickly dwindle and disappear.

Why Worship?

When we worship, our hearts are lifted to the
God who made the universe, a universe made
up of millions of galaxies, themselves each
made up of billions of stars and planets.

We dwell on one of those planets and our
sights are raised to the Trinity—to God the
Father and Creator; to the Son who is "the
radiance of God's glory and the exact
representation of his being, sustaining all
things by his powerful word," (Hebrews 1:3);
and to the Holy Spirit who was there at
creation bringing order out of chaos, and who is
with us now.

One of the primary aims of corporate prayer
must be to please God, and one of the best
means of achieving this is through worship.
Often, people may arrive at a prayer meeting
tired, distracted, or even discouraged. Then
they need to be helped to forget their anxieties
and to focus on God. We need to allow the Spirit
to lift us up and unite us with Christ from
where we can touch the Father's heart. Our

experience is that worship is an integral part of every meeting.

How to Organize Worship

First, a worship leader needs to be someone with a lead instrument (such as a guitar or piano), at least a few chords, and a love for God. With that combination, it has been wonderful to see people develop gifts in this area, often with little or no previous experience.

An example of this is Jamie Haith, who is now on the full-time staff of HTB as a worship leader. This is his account of what happened in 1992—shortly after he joined the church and began attending the Thursday evening prayer meeting.

I arrived to find that the worship was led without any instruments as there were no musicians at the meeting.

After a couple of weeks, I mentioned my three chords to Jeremy (feeling rather like the little boy with the fishes and the loaves) and before I could take it back he had asked me to bring along my guitar the next week.

To begin with, I concentrated on the

limited number of worship songs that I could play and, thankfully, the response was positive.

With time my repertoire expanded (much to everyone's relief!), and I became more confident in leading worship. It is one of the delights of my life now to be employed to do this very thing.

If you do not have a worship leader, there are alternatives such as saying a Psalm together or using prayers to thank and praise God. You can also sing to a tape or CD, and pray for the provision of a suitably gifted person in due course. What better way to receive an answer to prayer than when they appear!

Second, the relationship between the leader of the meeting and the worship leader is highly important. They need to trust and understand e a ch other. This will be made easier by working together regularly, and by meeting frequently to pray. Such a working relationship helps to enhance the quality of meetings as it develops.

Third, it is important to develop a continuous flow of praise. Song books which are arranged in alphabetical order, or an overhead projector, remove the need for stopping to announce song nu m b e r s. To signal the end of a time of prayer, the worship leader can begin to play a few chords and can indicate the restart of worship by saying something like "let's stand" if necessary.

Our meetings always start with an extended time of worship and then proceed with songs between most sections of prayer. Worship and prayer should be interwoven throughout. In this connection, there is also the model described in chapter 6, which involves half the people singing while the remainder pray at the same time.

Singing can also be an act of prayer in itself. Many songs are very powerful and beautiful prayers in themselves. Two examples, reproduced below, are "This Time Revival" by Andy Piercy and Charlie Groves and "Send Revival, Start with Me" by Matt Redman.

"This Time Revival"

Here we stand in total surrender,
lifting our voices,
abandoned to your cause.
Here we stand, praying in the glory,
of the one and only
Jesus Christ, the Lord.

This time revival,
Lord come and heal our land.
Bring to completion
the work that you've begun.
This time revival,
stir up your church again.
Pour out your Spirit
on your daughters and your sons.

Here we stand, in need of your mercy.
Father, forgive us
for the time that we have lost.
Once again, make us an army
to conquer this nation
with the message of the cross.

"Send Revival, Start with Me"

We're looking to your promise of old
that if we pray and humble ourselves,
you will come and heal our land.
You will come, you will come.

We're looking to the promise you made
that if we turn and look to your face,
you will come and heal our land.
You will come, you will come to us.

Lord, send revival, start with me,
for I am one of unclean lips,
and my eyes have seen the King.
Your glory I have glimpsed.
Send revival, start with me.[1]

Free Singing

It helps if the worship leader is confident about leading improvised singing. These can be beautiful times of worship and powerful prayer in their own right. The singing can be in our own language or in the Spirit and is often a mixture of both.

We had such a time at a prayer meeting during an Alpha conference once. We prayed that each delegate would receive all the blessings that God intended for them at the conference. After a while, the singing soared to a fresh height as the Spirit breathed new life into it and the process continued for quite a time. One couple said later that it was a highlight of the two days for them!

On another occasion, I remember a time of prayer for children. As the prayers died down, the worship leader started to sing a simple phrase relating to the theme. As the rest of us joined in, it became a moving time of further prayer. Such praying can often be prophetic in nature and brings with it the reminder that there are many different expressions of corporate prayer and worship.

Inspired Playing

I have never forgotten something I once heard the worship leader Graham Kendrick say: "The anointed playing of a musical instrument releases the Holy Spirit." For example, in 2 Kings 3, we read that Elisha requested a harpist to play when he had been summoned by the kings of Israel, Judah, and Edom to "inquire of the Lord" on their behalves concerning the outcome of their military campaign against Moab. As the harpist played, "the hand of the Lord came upon Elisha," (v. 15b), and he was able to foretell the means by which a wonderful deliverance and victory would be gained by the kings concerned.

We are finding that it can be very effective just to listen as our worship leader plays the piano (or other instrument) to us freely. At such times, there can be a powerful sense of God's presence, and this often proves to be the inspiration for a time of prophecy.

At two recent larger meetings, we have been

joined by a team of drummers, and they brought a new dimension to the worship and prayer. Sometimes, the drumming accompanied the other instruments and our singing; sometimes it reinforced times of corporate praying aloud; at other times it took place alone. There is something very dynamic and exciting about drums and they complemented the other activities and enhanced the meetings concerned.

Conclusion

The importance of worship in prayer meetings cannot be overstated. In response to it, and by His grace, God may sometimes give those involved a wonderful sense of His presence and a small glimpse of heaven on earth.

Note

1. Matt Redman, *Send Revival, Start with Me* 1996 Kingsway's Thankyou Music

CHAPTER 6

What about Different Models?

"Rend your heart and not your garments."
(Joel 2:13a)

Prayer meetings can be boring. My "amen" to someone else's prayer may lose some of its validity if my mind has been wandering during it! Furthermore, praying does not come naturally to many of us and we need help to become more effective at it. To address this requires imagination. A variety of ways of praying together helps maintain the enthusiasm of those who come week by week.

Before I outline any models of prayer, however, I want to stress that what concerns God is the cry of our hearts and not some special technique being used. Praying one by one in turn is probably the most familiar pattern at prayer meetings and is an effective way to pray together. However, we quickly realized, as the numbers at our meetings began to increase, that it also distinctly limits how much those present can pray. That, and the desire for more variety, led us to develop other models of corporate prayer including those which I will now describe.

Small Groups

The leader of the meeting could announce the topic for prayer by saying something like: "Now we are going to pray for the services on Sunday. Could you please get into groups of three or four to pray?" All we have done is to divide one larger group into a number of smaller ones and, at a stroke, the potential amount of prayer is multiplied. In each of these small groups, individuals will pray in turn. After a suitable period, the leader will direct the meeting into its next phase, or the worship leader can begin the next song, allowing people to join in as their individual prayers draw to a close.

If a person has never prayed out loud in public before, this is about the easiest setting in which to make a start. We often use it in the first section of a meeting as it helps those present to "get going."

The Acts 4 Model

This model involves everyone praying out loud together simultaneously and can be quite a culture shock when you first encounter it! There is a description of such prayer given in Acts 4: 23-30. In countries such as South Korea, it is often used at very large prayer meetings but it is effective in smaller ones as well. The leader, having introduced the topic to be prayed for, will direct those present to pray in this way and, following his or her lead, that is what they do. Some people feel inhibited by praying aloud with others, and we would always say that they are free to pray silently. Once we got used to it, this method proved very popular in our prayer meetings and we now use it regularly. Such times of prayer flow naturally into singing.

Dr. Paul Yonggi Cho, the Pastor of the Yoido Full Gospel Church of Seoul, Korea, introduced a time of such prayer at Wembley Arena by saying that, in his country, they often start by saying "Lord, Lord, Lord" together, and that is what 12,000 of us then did! It led to a dynamic time of prayer for London.

The Acts 4 model enables any group to maximize its potential for prayer because it involves everyone. It is perfectly possible to sustain it in sections of up to five minutes (though normally they are shorter than that). At larger meetings, the leaders can use the microphone to inject fresh impetus as it proceeds. This model also lends itself to issues about which the participants are likely to feel strongly—such as the development of God's work in prisons, or a new church plant, or some national or international crisis. Once experienced, you realize what a powerful means of prayer it can be. One way to pray for two topics at once is to ask the men to pray for one and the women to pray for the other, with both groups raising their voices together.

The Spirit seems to be guiding the Church to this type of prayer and blessing it. In continents as diverse as Asia and South America, where the church is growing rapidly, prayer meetings using such models are held. It is always a challenge for the people of God to move with the Spirit, and one of the biggest issues facing the denominations in the West today is to move forward in the area of corporate prayer. Whenever the Lord tells us that He is doing a new thing, it is easy to rejoice until we ourselves are confronted with change!

There need be nothing disorderly about such prayer. But it is exciting. After attending such a

meeting, the leader of one London church said,
"We were praying for revival. In my church if
we had a meeting like that, we would think
revival had come!"

Other Versions

Another version of the Acts 4 model involves
dividing the meeting into two parts. This is
normally each side of the room, although there
are other natural subdivisions, such as men
and women, so long as the two groups are
roughly balanced numerically. Again, the leader
of the meeting needs to make clear what is to be
prayed for next, explaining that the worship
leader will lead one side in singing while the
others pray out loud together. After a short
period, the roles are reversed, and it helps to
have identified a suitable person to give a lead
to each group. Frequently, we set the two sides
praying for different (often related) topics
thereby covering more ground in one section.
An exciting aspect of this model is the
interaction between worship and prayer.

This is the easiest way that I know to
introduce the concept of everyone praying out
loud together. There is no need for self-
consciousness on the part of the "pray-ers"

because the other half of the group are making a lively noise as they worship. We tend to let each side pray and worship for quite short periods before combining both in worship at the end of the section.

Some time ago, I received a letter from someone involved in starting a joint church prayer meeting, and part of it is reproduced below:

We have so far had four meetings—they are ecumenical and only once a month—and we are praying for church unity and preparing our area for outreach and evangelism. As our churches are all very traditional, we have been very gentle in what we have done, but last month we tried the model of half the people singing while the others prayed OUT LOUD. Some had never done this, but it worked well. People felt they had really been in touch with God.

We had fifteen people to the first meeting, and over the months others have come and gone because of the holiday period, so we have averaged about twenty. It's a start, and there's a growing feeling that a whole month is too long to wait for the next one.

We have now developed another form of the Acts 4 model, known to us as the "Prayer Sandwich"! It involves short sections of worship and prayer interspersed. For example, three separate topics can be prayed for with everyone praying aloud together, linked by a chorus or a single verse of worship between each section. This is helpful if a meeting is running out of time and there are still several outstanding matters to pray for. Alternatively, prayer for one topic could be divided by short times of worship. This creates further variety, though obviously the leader and worship leader must communicate closely if it is to work well. It can also be used if there are not enough people to divide the meeting into two parts in the way described above.

The Acts 4 model is also effective in sung form. This is described in the chapter on worship (under the heading "Free Singing"). It is quite an ambitious undertaking, but we need to be able to make mistakes. Without that freedom, it is impossible to make progress. Quite simply, if God seems to be blessing any prayer model (especially if that model has scriptural authority), we should reinforce it. Otherwise we must move on. Within this kind of framework, we can keep prayer meetings alive and exciting.

Other Models

Scriptural Proclamation

One of the most powerful things we can do in prayer meetings is to proclaim Scripture together. That is exactly what we do every time we pray the Lord's Prayer in a corporate context. The leader can direct those present to a relevant biblical passage and everyone then reads it aloud together, thus bringing the authority of the word of God to bear on a subject. Reading Scripture can also be a form of praise. In this regard, many Psalms are ideal and we have found that the passage from Philippians 2:6-11 reproduced below, starting with "Jesus" instead of "who" is very powerful when used in this way.

Jesus, being in very nature God, did not consider equality with God something to be grasped, but made himself nothing, taking the very nature of a servant, being made in human likeness. And being found in appearance as a man, he humbled himself and became obedient to death— even death on a cross! Therefore God exalted him to the highest place and gave him the name that is above every name, that at the name of Jesus every knee should bow, in heaven and on earth and under the earth, and every tongue confess that Jesus Christ is Lord, to the Glory of God the Father.

Anyone leading prayer meetings regularly can soon build up a collection of effective scriptural references for this purpose. It can be done by reading from the Bible (same version!) together or by using an overhead slide already prepared. This can be included at any time during the course of a meeting and will definitely reinforce the section concerned.

Praying for Individuals

One of the most constructive ways to focus prayer in a prayer meeting is through interviews. These are both interesting and useful in keeping church members informed about a wide range of activities. They may involve people who attend the meeting regularly, or who have been specially invited for the purpose. After the interview, those present can gather around the person (or people) concerned to pray for them and their work. We tend to do this by praying one at a time, followed by a time of praying aloud together for them. For example, we sometimes interview leaders of one of our church home groups. In that way, we hear how things are going, find out about activities the group is undertaking and, of course, receive requests for prayer.

The same format can be used to pray for members of other churches who are working in Christian positions, either locally or even overseas. Such prayer can help galvanize a meeting, build unity, and hopefully enhance the work of those concerned!

Cascade Principle

A very effective way to pray for a nation or any organization is to pray for its leaders, and Paul specifically encourages such prayers in 1 Timothy 2: 1-2. So one way to pray for a church is to pray for its pastor, believing that if he or she is blessed, then there will be a benefit to the whole church—the cascade effect.

On the national scale in England, the principle would be to pray for the Queen as Head of State, perhaps concentrating on issues such as her family, her leadership, or her role in the Church of England. Alternatively, this type of prayer could be focused on the Prime Minister as head of the government. In the United States, of course, the focus would be on the President.

Silent Prayer

The previous models can be quite noisy. As a contrast, silence can be very effective at a prayer meeting. The leader simply announces what is to be prayed for and that those present should allow the Spirit to guide them in a time of silent prayer.

This method of prayer proved invaluable on one particular occasion. About 120 of us were on a London river boat and had planned to pray for the government when we reached the Palace of Westminster. Having been warned by a friendly policeman that our representatives do not like being disturbed from the River Thames, we knelt and prayed using the silent model!

The leader must judge how long the silence should continue, and I do not think it is unspiritual for us to keep an eye on our watches. A period of sixty seconds can be very effective, but is surprisingly hard to judge.

Longer periods of silence can also allow time for contemplation and listening to God.

Summary

- Praying in Turn
- Small Groups—praying as above
- The Acts 4 Model
   a) praying aloud together
   b) Combined worship and prayer
   c) free singing
- Scriptural Prodamation—saying a passage from the Bible together
- Prayer for Individuals—preceded by interview
- Cascade Principle—prayer for leaders
- Silent Prayer

CHAPTER 7

What about Different Meetings?

*"You who call on the Lord, give yourselves no rest,
and give him no rest till he establishes Jerusalem
and makes her the praise of the earth."*
(Isaiah 62:6b-7)

The development of corporate prayer is a journey, and our experience is that the Holy Spirit has nudged us on step by step, often urging us to start a new phase just as we have begun to feel comfortable. My purpose in this chapter is to encourage the imaginative development of other prayer opportunities in addition to the regular prayer meetings in the life of a church. For us, one-hour meetings each week are at the heart of our corporate prayer, and the special events and meetings described below developed out of them, and could only operate alongside them. Not all these examples may work in every setting, but they are designed to show that there is a lot of potential for creativity when people pray together.

Prayer Weekends

When someone suggested praying for an entire weekend, my heart sank and my spirit rose simultaneously! How on earth would we do it? But, we felt God was in it and "Prayer Weekends" were born at HTB. We held our first in 1994, and we billed it with the logo: *"Let's Change the News."* As things turned out, the news did change, but in a totally unforeseen way. A few months later, there were stories in the media of people lining up to get into church and some very lively services. God was on the move and suddenly *that* was the news!

Since then, we have tried to organize one Prayer Weekend a year. So far, we have had three, with 175 people attending the last one. A sample program for a prayer weekend is shown on the next pages.

PRAYER WEEKEND

Friday

7:30 p.m. - 9:00 p.m.	Supper
9:00 p.m.	Short introduction

Saturday

7:00 a.m. - 8:00 a.m.	Personal prayer
8:30 a.m.	Breakfast
9:30 a.m. - 11:00 a.m.	**Main Session I**
9:30 a.m. - 10:15 a.m.	Worship/introductory talk
10:15 a.m. - 11:00 a.m.	Prayer and worship
11:00 a.m. - 11:30 a.m	Coffee
11:30 a.m. - 1:00 p.m.	**Main Session II** (Time divided into three half-hour slots of corporate prayer with different leaders for each section)
1:00 p.m.	Lunch
2:00 p.m. - 4:30 p.m.	Free time
4:30 p.m. - 5:00 p.m.	Tea
5:00 p.m. - 6:00 p.m.	Personal prayer
6:00 p.m. - 10:00 p.m.	**Main Session III**
6:00 p.m. - 6:30 p.m.	Worship and introductory talk
6:30 p.m. - 7:00 p.m.	Prayer for church leaders

7:00 p.m. - 7:30 p.m.	Prayer for more prayer at every level, such as personal, small group, church, etc.
7:30 p.m. - 8:00 p.m.	Prayer for life "at home" such as home groups, services, worship, etc.
8:00 p.m. - 8:30 p.m.	Worship/space for prophecy
8:30 p.m. - 9:00 p.m.	Prayer for London
9:00 p.m. - 9:30 p.m.	Prayer for Alpha and evangelism
9:30 p.m. - 10:00 p.m.	Prayer for revival Again, each half-hour slot led by a different leader and interspersed with worship.We miss the evening meal, but food is always provided for anyone for whom fasting would not be sensible.)
10:00 p.m.	Hot chocolate and cookies

Overnight

11:00 p.m. - 9:00 a.m.   Prayer watches (five two-hour slots each led by different leaders with attendance by rotation)

Sunday

9:00 a.m.   Breakfast

10:30 a.m. - 12:00 p.m.   **Main Session IV** (Including reports from prayer watches, worship and corporate prayer, informal communion, and praying for each other)

1:00 p.m.   Lunch and depart at leisure

5:00/7:30 p.m.   **Main Session V** - attend evening service at HTB. (This engenders an added sense of unity and celebration after a job well done!)

NOTE: All activities are optional.

All of these activities can be set against a background of twenty-four hours of continuous prayer. At our most recent prayer weekend, such a time ran from 11 a.m. on Saturday to 11 a.m. on Sunday. When organized prayer sessions were not already taking place on the program, groups of volunteers prayed together. At the end of the twenty four hours, we felt we had accomplished something new and significant.

Prayer weekends are a combination of a lot of fun and hard work. One report from a prayer watch on our first weekend was that for an hour and three quarters "it felt like wading through syrup" until they had a wonderful sense of God's presence in the last fifteen minutes. I was on the next watch, and we had an amazing time throughout, feeling that the ground had already been prepared for us.

Weekends involve a lot of organization, but they provide great opportunities for concentrated prayer. They also develop a strong sense of unity. There is a cost in terms of time and money, so once a year may be about right. One way to help people is to offer to subsidize the cost if necessary and to hold a collection on Sunday morning with the aim of covering this. An alternative to a Prayer Weekend could be a

Saturday "at home" with a suitably modified program.

Printed below is part of a letter I received from someone who attended one such weekend. The writer describes how she was healed in the ministry time on Sunday morning:

I've had a muscular condition (Fibro-myalgia) for fourteen years and in the last three years it has been severe. I've had to give up cooking as a profession and wear arm braces every night. Over the weekend my wrists had been swollen and bruised and extremely painful.

Somebody prayed for me and I felt heat in my arms. As the afternoon wore on I realized that the swelling and pain had gone from my wrists. I've monitored my arms since then and put them to the test—vacuuming, lifting the baby, shopping, and things that usually cause me a lot of pain—NOTHING! No swelling, no pain, nothing—praise God!

Prayer Celebrations

Our aim on these occasions is to reproduce the kind of session that we have found so effective on the Saturday evening of the prayer weekend. The meeting could start, for example, at 7:00 p.m. and end at 10:00 p.m., designed to allow people to recover from work and eat if they want to before it, and to get home afterward at a reasonable hour. The program begins with worship and a short introductory talk. The remainder of the time is then divided into half-hour sections led by different people, working through topics agreed upon in advance. Again the prayer is interspersed with worship, and the various models described in chapter 6 are used. We might include topics such as:

Sunday services
Home groups and other pastoral activities
Worship
Alpha
Families and relationships
Other churches
Youth and children
Homeless and unemployed
Prison work/teams *
Royal Family and government
Peace in Northern Ireland
National revival

*On one occasion, we were joined by the Chaplains of Lewes and Dartmoor prisons. It was very moving to hear stories of what God had been doing in these prisons and then to be able to pray for them and the spread of this work.

We aim to hold such meetings three times a year and they have now grown to a membership of 300-500 (obviously they need good publicity in advance). There always seem to be lots of visitors including people from overseas. God seems to like it when different elements of His family come together to pray and worship. We see such meetings as an ideal context in which to pray for revival. After a recent one, someone commented:

Prior to the meeting, I had been wondering how worthwhile prayer was (!) bearing in mind God knows what we are going to pray before we pray it, etc. While at the meeting, I looked out over everybody praying and thought again, "Is there any point to all of this?" As I was thinking this, I had an impression of God looking down from heaven and I knew that He was pleased with us and that He was listen-

ing to us. A split second later, Jeremy approached the microphone and told us that he felt the Lord had given him permission to say that "we had His ear." I knew then that there was a point to it all and that we were making a difference.

Days of Prayer

This is another experiment we have tried. We held our 7:00 a.m. regular prayer meeting, the theme for the day being Revival in London. People left for their normal day's activity after the meeting but were encouraged to fast and pray at lunch time, either individually or in small groups. We then reconvened at 7:00 p.m. to re-focus our prayers in the type of meeting already described. The meeting in the evening seemed to have a new dimension of power to it as a result of the prayer and fasting earlier in the day.

All-Night Prayer Meetings

These are a logical development of the Friday night prayer meetings. It has involved starting at 10:00 p.m. and praying through to 6:00 a.m. followed by a full cooked breakfast! The basic structure is again the same. We would always begin with worship followed by an introductory talk. The point of the talk is more to inspire people and to help them focus their minds than to teach. After welcoming everyone (especially visitors), I would take a short passage from the Bible, such as 2 Chronicles 7:13-14 or Joel 2:13, as the basis of my opening remarks. Then we pray.

Again, we have found that it is essential to break all-night prayer into sections with different leaders. I would suggest a structure along the following lines:

Hours
Worship/introduction
(more worship, less introduction)

1.0 Three separate main sections led by different leaders of one and a half hours each with the normal mix of worship and prayer

4.5 One section sub-divided into a variety (say four) of smaller meetings in different rooms with pre-determined subject matter and leaders leaving people to choose between the meetings for themselves

2.0 One section of worship and space for prophesy

0.5 Of course, there should always be plenty of room to maneuver. Leaders of the different sections need to bring all the inspiration they can (such as video clips, slides, background information, etc.), and it is this hard work carried out in preparation that makes all the difference in the meeting. That, together with good leadership, will greatly help to release people in their praying.

To keep going through the night, we need all the help we can get—including tea and coffee and exciting ways to pray. At one meeting recently, we arranged a livelink by telephone with the leaders of a church in Dublin at 5:00 a.m. Hearing from and praying together with our Dublin friends over the telephone revived us for the final stretch, making it easier to reach the cooked breakfast at 6:00 a.m.!

Also, more extended prayer meetings obviously allow time for more extended periods of worship.

Prayer Boats

I appreciate that this form of meeting requires living near water! The important point is

getting out into our communities to pray and
that can also be achieved on foot, in cars, or by
some other suitable form of transport. Anyway,
as London is on the River Thames, it occurred
to us in 1995 that an imaginative way to pray
for it would be from a river boat. Much of the
life of our capital city is represented along the
banks of its river. So *from* the heart of London
we were able to pray *for* the heart of London.

With about 120 people on board, we
embarked at Charing Cross Pier, passing St.
Paul's Cathedral, the Monument, the Tower of
London, the Express Newspaper Building,
Waterloo Bridge, Battersea Power Station, and
the Houses of Parliament before we returned
and disembarked at Charing Cross Pier. We
used these points to pray for the church, the
city, the Royal Family, the media, the homeless,
a large Christian venue for London, and for the
government. The various different prayer
models all worked on a boat and, with a
worship band on board, we worshiped as we
moved to the respective prayer points.

The whole journey lasted about three hours,
and it proved a most effective way to pray for
London. The banks of the river, lit up at night,
provide many beautiful sights, and are steeped
in history. Having our prayer subjects in sight

helped us to pray, and, again, we had different leaders for the various sections. No one was seasick or fell overboard, and we returned rejoicing!

More recently, we have completed a second prayer boat trip. This was similar to the first, but with a bigger boat and nearly three hundred people on board. Twice during the evening, we divided into two groups. A number decided to remain on the lower deck to worship. On the upper deck the others chose to pray for different issues. They gathered around several banners each connected with a different topic, and they prayed in sight of a related building. For example, those who wanted to pray for healing did so as the boat passed St. Thomas' Hospital.

New Year's Eve Prayer Parties

Toward the end of 1995, we decided to see in the New Year with a "Prayer Party." I must admit that my hopes were not very high but I was proved completely wrong. Lots of people came to the meeting from 10:00 p.m. to midnight which was followed by appropriate seasonal refreshments! This year, we extended the time by beginning at 9:00 p.m. and other "firsts" included more extended worship (and drumming), a time for prophecy, and a section of prayer during which color images set to music were shown to illustrate the themes. There were about five hundred people involved and many of us have now concluded that this is the best possible way to see in the New Year. We appreciate that we have joined a well-established tradition in this.

Theme Meetings

Sometimes, it can be very effective to devote the whole of a meeting to one major issue. We held such a meeting to pray for South Africa before the general election that brought President Mandela into office. There was expert opinion at the time that violence and loss of life were inevitable. I remember how thrilled we were when the elections passed by peacefully.

On another occasion, Deirdre Hurst, who is one of the regular prayer leaders at HTB, prepared and led a theme meeting for rain in Zimbabwe. The country was in acute drought and this is Deirdre's own record of the event.

It is difficult to prove cause and effect— nonetheless, when coincidences happen, we love to believe that God has answered our prayers.

One such experience happened in the autumn of 1995. A team from HTB had been in Zimbabwe at an Alpha conference in September and had seen the drought conditions there. The rainy season had been supposed to start at the end of August, but there had only been a few light showers instead of the heavy rain the country needed. Direct news of the drought continued to come to HTB through a member of our congregation, whose family comes from Zimbabwe. People were praying, of course, but, because the drought had continued, it seemed more prayer was needed.

As a result, we called a prayer meeting to pray for rain. We determined to be bold and cry out to the Lord for the rains to come. We prayed using a combination of praise and worship and different models of prayer. We used a map of Zimbabwe to help people focus and be specific in their prayer.

It was only a couple of days later that we heard the news from Zimbabwe that the rains had started—the heavy rain that the country needed. We know many other people had been praying and we certainly don't believe that there was anything extra special about our prayers but perhaps we had been allowed to make some small contribution to the Lord's overall scheme of things.

More recently we had a "theme meeting" to pray for peace in Northern Ireland. On such occasions, it helps to remind ourselves that this is not about our strength or what we can do. We need to focus on the One to whom our prayers are addressed and what He can do. The issues (whatever they are) then seem much more manageable!

Summary

- Prayer Weekends
  a) at a residential center
  b) a Saturday "at home"
- Prayer Celebrations—an extended time in the evening of prayer and worship
- All Night Prayer Meetings—praying through the night
- Prayer Boats—going out into the community to pray

- New Year's Eve Prayer Parties—praying in the New Year
- Theme Meetings—devoting a whole meeting to one issue

CHAPTER 8

What about the Future?

*"Oh, that you would rend the heavens
and come down ..."* (Isaiah 64:1a)

On January 4, 1990, I believe God showed me
something of His plans for the coming years. It
was early in the morning and I was praying.
Although I wasn't expecting anything unusual,
I had what seemed to be a vision. In it, I saw
sheets of rain falling vertically onto very dry
and parched ground. The rain at first bounced
off the surface because of its dryness to a height
of about six inches. Then it fell back to the
ground and began to soak into it. I also had an
impression of a plow plowing up the middle of
our country, turning over the old soil and
leaving the new exposed.

I believe the vision spoke of a spiritual
drought in our nation coming to an end. It

seemed to represent God pouring out His Holy Spirit on a massive scale. As the rain soaked in, it appeared to be washing the soil, which I sensed related to a time of forgiveness and healing. We have a lot to repent of in the church and nationally.

The impression of the plow suggested that we should allow the new life that God longs to bring to His church to come to the surface and to grow. Since then we have seen a new outpouring of the Holy Spirit, profoundly affecting the lives of many churches. There are other encouraging signs of life including the spread of the Alpha course, the growing movement of God in our nation's prisons, the new hunger for prayer, and thousands of Christians uniting for events like March for Jesus.

My aim in this book has been to encourage every reader to see that dynamic, exciting, and productive corporate prayer should be central to the life of their church. If you are thinking of starting it, my advice is to start small and think big, and then, who knows what might be achieved over the next ten years? One exciting aspect of most of the prayer models described in this book is that they can work at any level from a few people upward. They are, therefore, appropriate to the various groups that make up most churches. I don't know how the journey of corporate prayer will develop, but I do know that there is still a long way to go. The goal is the fulfillment of the words, "Thy kingdom come, Thy will be done on earth as it is in heaven."

Only with prayer can we hope to see the healthy church and society that we long for. I believe that God plans to release His power in our land on a scale we have not witnessed before. Our response, surely, is to say "Yes Lord" with all our united heart and strength. Once we have done this, it will be hard to stop praying until God completes His work. Like Isaiah, our cry needs to become: "Oh, that you would rend the heavens and come down..." (Isaiah 64:1a). Dynamic prayer in the local church must be a vital part of this. After all, the church is the only army on earth that finds victory on its knees.

If you are interested in finding out more about resources or your nearest Alpha course, please contact:

Alpha U.S.A.
74 Trinity Place
New York, NY 10006
Tel: 888.949.2574
Fax: 212.406.7521
e-mail: info@alphausa.org
www.alphausa.org

Alpha Canada
1620 W. 8th Ave., Suite 300
Vancouver, BCV6J 1V4
Tel: 800.743.0899
Fax: 604.224.6124
e-mail: office@alphacanada.org
www.alphacanada.org

To purchase resources in Canada:

Cook Communications Ministries
P.O. Box 98, 55 Woodslee Avenue
Paris, ONT N3L 3E5
Tel: 800.263.2664
Fax: 800.461.8575
e-mail: custserv@cook.ca
www.cook.ca